FIND YOUR POWER

NUMEROLOGY

An Hachette UK Company
www.hachette.co.uk

First published in Great Britain in 2023 by Godsfield,
an imprint of Octopus Publishing Group Ltd
Carmelite House, 50 Victoria Embankment, London EC4Y 0DZ
www.octopusbooks.co.uk

ISBN 978-1-8418-1538-1

A CIP catalogue record for this book is available from the British Library

Printed and bound in China

10 9 8 7 6 5 4 3 2

Publisher: Lucy Pessell
Designer: Isobel Platt
Senior Editor: Hannah Coughlin
Assistant Editor: Samina Rahman
Production Controller: Allison Gonsalves
Illustration: p.13 Golden Spiral created by Zach Bogart
from the Noun Project

FIND YOUR POWER

NUMEROLOGY

KITTY GUILSBOROUGH

GODSFIELD

CONTENTS

FIND YOUR POWER

When daily life becomes busy and your time and energy is pulled in many different directions, it can be difficult to find time to nourish yourself. Prioritizing your own wellbeing can be a struggle and you risk feeling overwhelmed, unsure of where to turn and what you need in order to feel lighter and find your inner strength.

Taking some time to focus on yourself, answering questions you may be avoiding or facing problems that are simmering away under the surface is the best gift you can give yourself. But it can be difficult to know where to start.

Sometimes all you need to learn life's big lessons is a little guidance. In this series of books you will learn about personal healing, self empowerment and how to nourish your spirit. Explore practices which will help you to get clear on what you really want, and that will encourage you to acknowledge – and deal with – any limiting beliefs or negative thoughts that might be holding you back to living life to your fullest power.

These pocket-sized books provide invaluable advice on how to create the best conditions for a healthier, happier, and more fulfilled life Bursting with essential background, revealing insights and useful activities and exercises to enable yourself to understand and expand your personal practices every day, it's time to delve into your spiritual journey and truly Find Your Power.

Other titles in the series:

- *Find Your Power: Manifest*
- *Find Your Power: Tarot*
- *Find Your Power: Runes*

INTRODUCTION TO NUMEROLOGY

The universe reveals itself to us in numbers.

This statement is, somehow, both spiritually and practically true: one of the rare occasions when the scientist and the occultist may be in absolute agreement. The universe is made sense of through numbers. We search for data; we interpret the data; we know a little more. We go again. How do we know about far-off galaxies, about the tiniest atom? We know because we can run the numbers. We can run the numbers to launch a rocket, or to magnify something minuscule a million times. With numbers, we can make the invisible visible; the impossible possible. We can begin to understand the infinite.

There are places where science and spirituality converge, and this is one such place: the magic of numbers, and the mystery that numbers can reveal.

But perhaps, like many of us, you're not over-fond of numbers. Perhaps you were never great at maths at school, and you're pretty pleased to have left it behind in the classroom. Perhaps now numbers mostly mean money; and money mostly – if you're anything like the majority of people – means stress. Perhaps numbers just seem a little bit dry – and not what you were hoping to find in here. But stay with me. Something compelled you to open this book – perhaps even just the price. Maybe three little numbers printed on the back that made it seem worth your while; and maybe those numbers told

The stars have aligned to bring us here together.

you something important. Maybe they told you that this book was for you, or could be for you. Maybe it's payday. Maybe it's your lunchbreak, or a weekend; the day or the time when you've got a moment to yourself. Maybe it's just added up right: you're here, and I'm here. The stars have aligned, even briefly, to bring us here together on page 10. And you think, maybe, I'm being flippant. You think that numerology isn't about money, and you're right: it's about much more than that. Numbers have much more to say than just cold, hard cash.

2

NUMBERS MAKE THE WORLD GO ROUND

But there's a reason I'm starting here. I'm starting here to remind you that numbers are everywhere, and numbers are important.

Numbers are everywhere, and numbers are important.

In fact, they've never been more important than right now: think of social security, your mobile digits, and all the ones and zeros of a million computer systems. Numbers run our lives; they tell us who we are, and what we can do, and where we can go. The numbers in our bank account. The numbers on our passport. The numbers of our postal code, even, determine where we go to school and how much our homes might cost and what our vote is worth. Numbers make the world go round.

And let's be clear: these numbers are arbitrary, for sure. They are constructs. But so is everything. So are words. So are stories.

And there are stories in numbers: stories that make sense of the universe, and stories that make the universe go round.

Literally, in some cases. Here's a story in numbers for you.

THE FIBONACCI
SEQUENCE

The Fibonacci Sequence is a series of numbers in which each number is the product of the two that came before. If we start with 0 + 1, we get 1. If we add 1 and 1, we get 2. If we add 2 and 1, we get 3. 3+2 = 5; 5+8 =13; 8+13 = 21; 13+21 = 34 and so on, all the way to infinity. If we draw this out on squared paper, we get something that looks like this.

This is what's called a perfect spiral, which increases exactly proportionately to itself.

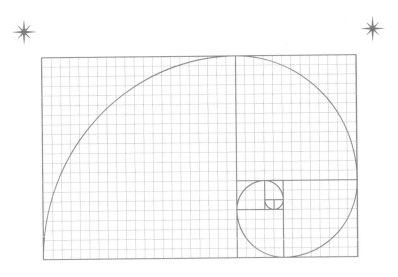

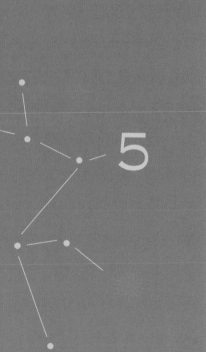

And here's the interesting thing: this perfect spiral shows up everywhere in nature. This perfect spiral, and this perfect number sequence, shows up way more than you might think. This series of numbers was first discovered as the answer to a puzzle about the breeding habits of rabbits, 800 years ago, but it also appears when we look at things like tree branches and beekeeping and storm clouds. A bee colony increases itself in this pattern; a tree grows to this pattern; and storm clouds? Hurricanes, like galaxies, arrange themselves into this perfect spiral.

So, too, does the human ear. It shows up in the way sunflower seeds arrange themselves in the heart of the flower. It shows up in the way pine cones arrange their ridges. It shows up in shells, if you cut them in half: each new chamber in the nautilus shell is equal to the

Numbers tell a story of what it is to be alive.

size of the two before it combined. Some call it "God's rule for growing things". Others, more boldly, "God's fingerprint". We don't know why it's the same everywhere. We don't know what it means. But we know it shows us that everything is connected.

These numbers – known as the Sacred Geometry, the Golden Ratio and many other names beside – tell a story of what it is to be alive. Or, more broadly, what it is to exist. The numbers have meanings, and they map onto our observed experience to tell us something: to show us things that might not otherwise have been apparent, to show us that everything is one.

When we find the numbers, we find the truth.

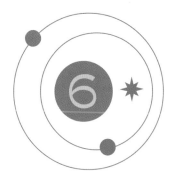

THE POETICS
OF NUMBERS

Numbers might be a construct, but they are a construct made of people, and made by people, and they are stories in and of themselves. We count in Base-10 – which is to say, we count in multiples of ten – because we have ten fingers. Mathematically speaking, it might be better if we had 12 fingers, and counted in Base-12. Computers count in Base-2, binary code, with only ones and zeros. But we count in Base-10, because we have ten fingers. It is as simple as that. We look down at our hands, and find out how to use them to bring the universe together. The pattern of our fingers shapes the way we shape the universe: we see what makes sense in ourselves and send that sense out to bear order on the chaos of the cosmos.

We make systems out of what we have, and use those systems to understand the incomprehensible: we make meaning from the meaningless, and stories out of stardust. That is being a scientist; that is being a spiritualist. That is being a person.

This is never truer than when we start to study numerology. Numerology is, in some ways, a poetics of numbers: it looks for patterns and shapes and textures in figures the way a poet might look for rhyme and assonance and alliteration in words. And we use what we find to bring meaning and shape to our lives. Just like with a poem.

And yet, somehow, numerology is maybe the most maligned inhabitant of the fortune-telling family. Not as mainstream as horoscopes, not as picturesque as the Tarot and with none of the classic charm of the palmist's art, the magic of arithmancy is out of fashion these days. And yet, with a little time, it can be the most rewarding of all.

> **Numerology is a poetics of numbers; it looks for patterns and shapes in figures.**

The numerology you will find in this book draws on a variety of sources – because numerology has been practised all over the world, and for thousands of years. There is no one way to practise numerology, and no one way to interpret a single number: for instance, seven is lucky in the global West, and not so lucky in the global East. In China, phone numbers are often for sale at different prices depending on how many eights they contain (auspicious!); but in Christian countries, a phone number containing "666" (the number of the beast!) might put off all but the very bold.

Seven is the number of deadly sins, but it's also the number of wonders of the world, days of the week and colours of the rainbow – if you're speaking English. Isaac Newton, who first identified the workings of the rainbow, saw only six colours there. Most cultures see only six colours in a rainbow. But we call it seven. Why? Because Newton thought seven just made more sense. He added in "indigo", somewhere between blue and violet, to fit in with a long tradition of sacred sevens – and now that's part of scientific fact. We teach our children that Richard of York Gave Battle in Vain – or whatever mnemonic you use – because seven felt right to Isaac Newton. Seven made sense to him. The musical scale has seven notes, he said, and there should be a colour for each note.

Of course, different countries use different scales. Perhaps in a universe where Newton grew up listening to chords on the pentatonic scale, with five notes in it, he might have simply condensed blue and purple into one. We shape our reality based on our beliefs; we make meaning out of everything, because people are meaning-making machines.

We shape our reality based on our beliefs; we make meaning out of everything.

THE BOUBA OR KIKI EFFECT

And yet the relationship between language and reality goes both ways.

There is a very famous experiment called the "bouba/kiki effect" in which groups of people – everyone from Tamil-speaking students to English-speaking toddlers – are presented with two shapes.

One of these shapes is named "bouba". One is "kiki". Which is which? Most people know instantly that the sharp shape is "kiki", and the soft shape is "bouba". Even toddlers can pick this up. Because language, while a construct, comes from something deep inside us. Language is arbitrary, but it comes from somewhere real; names are arbitrary, numbers are arbitrary, but so is life. And life is what we make of it.

This book is about what we make of life. It's about how we go through life; and it's about the journey that begins on the day we're born, and ends the day we die. It's about the ways we choose, and the obstacles that are chosen for us. It's about the luck that's granted to us, and the prayers that are answered, and the ones that aren't. It's about the shape of our lives.

We do not, perhaps, choose the paths we walk. But we can always choose how we will walk them.

Bouba

Kiki

TRANSLATING
THE CHAOS

There are lots of ways to calculate the numbers that mean something to you.

You might simply notice a number occurring frequently in your life – your house number, your partner's birthday, the randomly assigned number on the back of your football shirt. Some numbers might just feel right to you: lucky numbers, you might say. Something calls to you, or simply emerges. The pattern makes itself visible to you. And yet there are other patterns, too, harder to see but no less crucial.

There are a lot of numbers that mean something to you – from the hour of your birth right down to your postal code or phone number – and a lot of ways to interpret them. Playing with numbers is like playing with the fabric of the universe, and it's a game as old as the gods. Early religious texts and mythological stories are full of ways we can interpret numbers

to unpick the secrets within – and not just numbers. We can also use these systems to translate words, like your name, into numbers, too. These kind of translations from letters into numbers – and from complex numbers to a simple single digit, as we will see over the next few pages – are a translation from the specific to the universal.

We are attached, naturally, to the specifics of our own lives. We are attached to our own stories, and to ourselves as the main characters. We are capable of thinking of our lives as personal, private and ultimately lonely experiences. At worst, it can feel that we have to live alone in our own minds, falling through the unknown with no sense of where we should be going.

Ancient Buddhist theory teaches us that to achieve enlightenment, we must - in very simplistic terms - escape the prison of the self. Nirvana, pure peace, comes when we extinguish our attachment to the self: it comes when we understand that we are one with the universe, and the universe is one with us. We are part of the cosmos, made of same stuff as stars and ashes and deep earth, and our stories are not original. Our stories are our own, certainly, but they belong to a universal pattern of human experience: we all want to live, love, and be loved. Remember that universal teenage lament: nobody understands me! What might it be like to accept that we were understood? What might it feel like to accept that we are seen - and known? How would it be if we chose to try to see where we fit into the pattern of the universe?

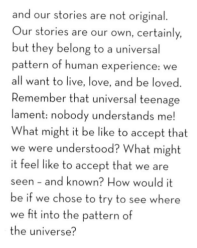

But it can be so hard to do this, even if we want to. It can be so hard to tune out the noise, and tune in to where we belong. We live in a world of so much information, and it can feel like so much chaos. We are so many complex things, and the world is even more messy: there are a million forces pulling us in every direction. It's impossible to reconcile everything around us with everything we are; and almost impossible to understand who we are, and where we should go. Who should we be? What should we do? What's for the best? It can be paralysing.

There's just so much going on, all the time, isn't there? There's so much to think about and do; so many elements to consider and prioritize and figure out.

So, what if we could refine it? What if we could be given a sense of who we are, and a map to where we should go? What if we could reconcile everything?

Our stories belong to a universal pattern of human experience.

7

TRUSTING THE SYSTEM

This, then, is numerology.

This is why numerology is so appealing. This is why it lasts.

Numerology is a system for converting everything – the chaos of the universe – around us into a single compatible language. We translate everything that really matters to the same language: that of numbers. We shift letters into numbers; and render numbers down to their single digit form. When we translate the disparate elements of our lives they can speak to each other: we can understand them in conversation with one another, and in tandem. We can simplify the chaos. We can tap in to a universal system, and find our place within it.

At a more advanced stage, of course, it's possible to do this with literally anything, anything at all. There are many different calculations possible – from adding up the vowels or consonants in your name, to the day of your birth, the year of your birth, or both.

In this modern world, two pieces of information define us above all others: our name, and our date of birth. They are given to us the moment we enter this world, and if we are lucky will be written over us long after we have left it. They make us the individuals we are, and yet they also are our passport to a wider system – literally. They simultaneously mark us out from the crowd, and let us be part of society. When we translate our name, we wind up with a Personality Number one way, and our Heart's Desire the other. When we translate our date of birth, we wind up with a Life Path Number.

To calculate each of these three numbers, we simply add each digit – or digit assigned to each letter – and keep adding until we reach one single figure. Each digit stands alone: there's no two or three digit numbers here. 45 isn't forty-five, it's four plus five. 237 isn't two hundred and thirty-seven: it's two plus three plus seven, which gives us twelve – which gives us one plus two, which gives us three.

MASTER NUMBERS

There's only one exception to this endless simplification: the so-called Master Numbers. These numbers are the alliterative numbers: 11, 22, and 33. Any doubled number is worth paying special attention to, but these three are particularly powerful. Simply expressed, they contain both the powers of the base digit and the sum of the doubled digit: both Magician and Dreamer, someone with the skills to communicate her dream to the world and make it live; both Dreamer and Master, pulling the magic of the moon into both the craft she works and those she teaches; both Storyteller and Goddess, spinning her fables into real life power.

These numbers don't just reduce directly down to 2, 4 and 6: they retain a power all their own, a power that magnifies the strength and struggles of their base numbers into something pure and astounding. The two numbers have double strength, and if you find one of these numbers in your birthdate or name, chances are there's something extra special about you. These are the numbers of the real big deal. These people make the world go round. These people change things up. If you find these numbers within your name or birthday, the strengths of that base digit goes double for you.

This formula, and these rules, are the same whether we're calculating Personality, Heart's Desire or Life Path, though each may of course give a completely different result.

Don't worry if you're still confused: we'll see some examples of these shortly.

NUMBERS IN LIFE

To put it in basic terms, the Personality number is how we walk through the world; the Heart's Desire is what calls to us along the way; and the Life Path is where we must walk. Our name gives us the key to who we are and what we might want; and our birthday to the journey on which we have been set. Let's unpack these a little bit. The relationship between these three numbers shapes the course of our lives. These three together shape what we do, and the feelings we have about everything that occurs: not just the actions we take, but the actions we let pass us by, the dreams we chase, and the dreams we hang on to.

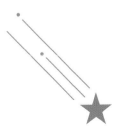

We can tap into a universal system and find our place within it.

PERSONALITY NUMBER

First, the Personality Number. This derives from the consonants of our name (more on this to come) and it's often the first thing we turn to in Numerology. Interestingly, it's the first thing people turn to, and it relates to the first things people see about you: your most obvious self, the self you present to company. It's the self that you use both as butler and bodyguard: come in, come in, but don't come too close.

3

Who we are is not a fixed construct. It changes through time, love and suffering.

This is who I am – and it's all I am. Don't look any harder. Don't dig any deeper. It's a protective self: it's a projected self. This number can tell us much of how we are perceived by the world – and perhaps even how we perceive ourselves. It can give us clues to the ways we might exist to others: it can open us up to the ways we come across and the ways we show ourselves to be. It tells us of who we are. Or, more accurately, it tells us of who we are in some ways.

It tells of who we have been, and not – and this is the crucial thing – of who we may be. For it often comes as a surprise to newcomers to Numerology that the Personality Number is not the most important of the three. You'd think that the Personality Number would define you, wouldn't you? You might think that who we are is the thing we're looking for here.

And yet who we are, you see, is not a fixed construct. It changes through time, through love, through suffering. It changes through joy and pain and want and need, through dreams lost and dreams fulfilled. Our sense of self expands and contracts to fill the space available – and even, sometimes, to push past it into the next thing. We can't escape the core self we're given, and it's as hard to shake off as a name: as shaping and formative as what's written on your birth certificate. And yet, it's not everything. Not by a long way. We're so much more than a name, and we're so much more than what we're given. What we want, and what we get, changes us.

HEART'S DESIRE

So let's turn now to the Heart's Desire number, or – in some traditions – the Soul's Urge number. This derives from the vowels of our name: the soft outbreath sounds of AEIOU carry our secret longings from the inner self to the outer world, and with it we learn a little more about what we're drawn to. Think of the way that vowel sounds are spoken without tension or hard ending: ah! oh! They are sounds that come unbidden, that spill from us whether we like it or not. They mark love and terror, surprise and pleasure: they are the secret self, the markers of desire. If the crisp consonants resolve into a Personality Number and the outer perspective, these soft vowels condense down into the Heart's Desire and the inner voice. What do we want? Who do we want? This is where we turn to understand the romantic elements of our life, and our relationships to our loves – not purely sexual, but so much more than that too. The people in our lives are often metaphors for the kind of person we want to be: our relationships are aspirational, in that a good relationship must always make us feel like our best self. What are we drawn to? What are we hoping for? What do we crave?

This Heart's Desire tells us what we want. It doesn't, however, tell us what we need.

These two numbers are the keys to who we appear to be and who we long to be. They unlock our inner and outer selves.

The heart's desire tells us what we want, but not what we need.

6

LIFE PATH NUMBER

Yet there's something else we need, too: as we learn who we are, we must also understand where we might be going. We need a destination. We need goals. And this, then, is where the Life Path comes in.

This is the crucial number. It is our choices, after all, that shape our lives over everything else. The Life Path number is all about choices: choices, goals, ideals and travels.

The Life Path number sets us on one of nine possible routes through life: it gives us one of nine tangible directions, nine tangible goals. The Life Path is a guide to a journey; and it is the journey we go on that gives our life shape, and gives the self – the self we were born with, the self we were given with our name – meaning. The Life Path is not a checklist, and it's not a prophecy: it's just a sense that if we try to walk with this as our guide, we will find satisfaction.

So let's go now, and look at how we calculate these three numbers. Let's find out what others think of us; and what we think of ourselves. And then let's find out where we're taking that self.

This book is arranged into nine chapters, of course, one for each digit. If you've studied numerology before, you might notice something a little different about this book: the names for those nine chapters.

There are so many possible names for each of the nine paths, but in this book, we've given each path the name of an archetype: a guide, or a friend.

Nine paths, nine story-shapes: nine figures to lead and guide you through life. They are drawn from many sources: Jungian dream analysis, mythological traditions, spiritual traditions, gods, goddesses and stories older than memory. And this is because everything is connected: if there's one thing we can learn from the Fibonacci Sequence (see page 12), it's that there are patterns in everything, and that to look at one thing in isolation is always foolish.

So here the Tarot deck, in which every number corresponds with a card of the Major Arcana, lends us her beauty. Astrology can lend us the wisdom of the universe. And of course, when you invoke the stars, you're also invoking a whole pantheon of gods and goddesses, of ancient knowledge and secret strength.

You will walk alongside the figure who champions your Life Path, but you are set on that way by the one who gives you your Personality. They may work together in harmony, but maybe not. Maybe the tension between the two figures has caused you strife in your life, or perhaps it has driven you to become who you are. Either way, by reading both perhaps you will come to a new understanding – and new understanding that leads to new openness, new freedom, and new peace.

It's hard to go through things by yourself; and it's surprisingly easy, especially these days, to feel a little lost. Life is a journey; and all our journeys are different. And yet, if we look closely, there are patterns in things. There are patterns, and nothing new under the sun: someone has always been there before us. Someone has struggled as we struggle, suffered as we suffer. We are never truly alone, on our journey. My hope is that these nine archetypes, whoever it is that speaks to and with you, can walk with you on your way. These archetypes will lead you through an almost-but-not-quite guided meditation; a series of thoughts, ideas and even exercises that may take you closer to reaching your full potential.

I cannot tell you who you are; I cannot tell you what choices you will make. I cannot make you do anything you don't want to do. You have free will here. But I can tell you the things that seem to me likely to befall you; and I can – I hope! – help you figure out how to overcome them. I can tell you: there is a river here, but maybe you can build a bridge there. There is a volcano ready to erupt right where you might hope to walk, but could we go the long way round instead? Sure: here be monsters; but here's a sword and shield (or, for the pacifists among us, some monster-taming treats).

The pages that follow are not instructions, but maps: maps, and a guide to walk with you. Turn to the guides that you most need, and find – I hope – some footsteps to follow, and a hand to hold.

The pages that follow are not instructions, but maps and your guide.

CALCULATING YOUR PERSONALITY NUMBER

WHAT'S IN A NAME?

You might think a name is arbitrary – and you might be right. Of course, we're assigned it by other people, and no matter how well they love us, they can't know everything about who we are. And especially not at the moment of naming. So a name is arbitrary, maybe.

But the consequences of a name are anything but. What's in a name? "A rose by any other name would smell as sweet," Juliet laments in Shakespeare's famous play – but we know that she's wrong. It's her name that dooms her marriage, and indeed her young life. She and her love, Romeo, have different surnames – and those two names tie them into a war that is much older than them both. And this isn't just something from the olden days, or from the theatre. We see these kinds of name-effects every day in real life too.

Studies have shown that our names have all kinds of practical, tangible effects on our lives – from the careers we have and where we live, to how easily we move through the world. Our names can influence how hard we study; and how likely we are to be interviewed for a job. Our names show others who we are, or at least, a facet of who we are: our background, our culture, our heritage. What we are given by others comes down, often, to our names. And not just that. Some scientists have even found that our names influence how we give to others. If your name begins with the same letter as that of a particular hurricane, you're actually more likely to donate to the relief efforts for that hurricane. Isn't that wild? Our names shape us; and here's a way we can begin to understand that.

Our names shape us and here's a way we can begin to understand that.

8

There are several systems for translating letters into numbers. We can start with a straightforward letter to number substitution system, where A=1, B=2, and all the way to Z=26 (making, when simplified, Z= 2+6= 8); but there are also more mystical systems, most famously Chaldean and Pythagorean.

In order to find the Personality Number, we will use only the consonants of our name. As discussed previously, whatever system you use, you'll simply take the corresponding number for each consonant, and add it up to get a total. Then, you'll rationalize that total down by adding up every digit in that total and continuing until you come to a single figure.

In order to find the Heart's Desire Number, we use only the vowels, and the same system holds true.

You'll turn then to the corresponding Path. It's not necessarily your Path to walk – but it will have resonance for you, nonetheless. In this way, you'll be able to see more clearly and sense more deeply the tensions in your life: are you perceived as a leader-figure Magician (Life Path #1), but your true calling is the caring Domestic Goddess (Life Path #6)? Are you living the life of the Domestic Goddess, running a beautiful home and taking care of your family, while spiritually longing for the lonely ascetic intelligence of the Hermit (Life Path #9)? Are you a Hermit drawn to the life of the Magician, longing for the recognition that it might bring you? A Dragon longing for a life less materialistic, like a Hermit? A Magician with a Master at her heart, but longing still for something wilder, stranger, more Free Spirited?

How do these things work together? How do they clash? How do they harmonize? How do they sing together, come together, spark and spark from one another to light your way?

And, furthermore, what space might you be able to grant yourself if you understood these tensions? What grace? What freedom? Could you give yourself permission, perhaps, to be kinder not only to the people around you, who might want what you can't give, but also to those private unvoiced desires?

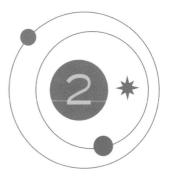

THE PYTHAGOREAN
METHOD

If you remember anything from high school maths, you probably remember the name Pythagoras, famous for his theorem and useful for triangles. This is that same Pythagoras – although it must be said that his connection to the theorem is somewhat lost to time. A sixth-century Greek, he lends his name not only to triangles but also to an ancient cult of numbers: the oldest cult of numerology for which we have clear records. The Pythagoreans believed in the power of numbers, and that each number corresponded to a planet (including, intriguingly, a secret tenth planet, hiding behind the sun, that was as special and magic as the number ten). They also were the first to discover the relationship between numbers and sounds that make up the whole of present-day music theory. Music exists in simple whole-number ratios to itself: in real terms, imagine a string on a violin. That makes a note; that note has a particular pitch. If you take a second string, exactly half as long, the note produced there will resonate in perfect harmony with the first. This is what's now called an octave; and the Pythagoreans also discovered musical fourths, musical fifths, and so on. In many ways, this now has wider scientific applications too – in things like string theory, the ideas we have about the beginnings and fabric of the universe itself.

So why does this matter to us? It matters because numerology is about exactly these connections, and understanding the ways numbers have real-world resonance. When we understand what the Pythagoreans believed about numbers – and the ways their ideas have been proved and continue to be proved true – we can take them seriously. We can take their translations seriously. On the next page you'll find one of the possible Pythagorean number charts: logical, straightforward, and useful.

Let's use the Pythagorean System to calculate the Personality Number and Heart's Desire Number for Scarlett Theodora Schwartz.

Numerology is understanding the ways in which numbers have real-world resonance.

PERSONALITY NUMBER

S + C + R + L + T + T + T + H + D + R + S + C + H + W + R + T + Z

1 + 3 + 9 + 3 + 2 + 2 + 2 + 8 + 4 + 9 + 1 + 3 + 8 + 5 + 9 + 2 + 8 = 79

7 + 9 = 16

1 + 6 = 7

HEART'S DESIRE NUMBER

A + E + E + O + O + A + A

1 + 5 + 5 + 6 + 6 + 1 + 1 = 25

2 + 5 = 7

1	2	3	4	5	6	7	8	9
A	B	C	D	E	F	G	H	I
J	K	L	M	N	O	P	Q	R
S	T	U	V	W	X	Y	Z	

What does this tell us about Scarlett? There's something sort of fascinating about a person who has the same inner and outer reality: a person who really means what they say, and starts as they mean to go on. Scarlett must turn to #7, The Searcher, to find her truth – but I think she probably already knows it. I don't think it will hold too many surprises for Scarlett, a person who carries herself with the knowledge that she's sincere all the way down.

When you consider that #7, The Searcher, is about the desire for deeper knowledge and perfect truth, we can consider that Scarlett might be uniquely well placed to begin her journey through life – and so, perhaps, she might now turn to her Life Path number to see where this searching personality will take her.

THE CHALDEAN SYSTEM

The Chaldean system was devised by the Irish mystic Cheiro, in the nineteenth century. Cheiro was incredibly famous, dealing with such luminaries as Oscar Wilde and Thomas Edison, and his system of palm reading gave rise to the alternative time "cheiromancy". He told the fortunes of the British Prime Minister Gladstone; and the actress Lillie Langtry; and even convinced Mark Twain to believe, just for a little while. "Chaldean" is an antiquated term for "Aramaic", as in the language family that gave rise to modern Hebrew – and is based on the Hebrew alphabet, rather than the Roman. This adds a whole new level of complication: Hebrew has twenty-two letters, and the Roman twenty-six, so you're effectively translating twice. It's based on the vibrations of the sound of each (Hebrew) letter, in relation to the vibrations of the sound of each (Hebrew) number. And if this sounds arcane to you, well – how arcane must the Pythagorean system have sounded two thousand years ago? And how right has it proved to be?

Let's use the Chaldean System to calculate the Personality Number and Heart's Desire Number for Victor Finnegan Green.

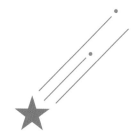

PERSONALITY NUMBER

V + C + T + R + F + N + N + G + N + G + R + N =

6 + 3 + 4 + 2 + 8 + 5 + 5 + 3 + 5 + 3 + 2 + 5 = 51

5 + 1 = 6

HEART'S DESIRE NUMBER

I + O + I + E + A + E + E =

1 + 7 + 1 + 5 + 1 + 5 + 5 = 25

2 + 5 = 7

1	2	3	4	5	6	7	8
A	B	C	D	E	U	O	F
I	K	G	M	H	V	Z	P
J	R	L	T	N	W		
Q		S		X			
Y							

What does this tell us about Victor? Well, we can see that by this system, he's not like Scarlett – but he'd like to be. In fact, he might be strongly drawn to Scarlett, who has the seeking, questing, eager energy he longs for. Does he seek her romantically? Does he seek to learn from her? It could be both; it could be either, or neither, but what's certain is that the powerful double energy of #7 she embodies is his Heart's Desire. But would she recognise that? Victor isn't putting the Searcher energy out into the world – what he's projecting is #6, The Domestic Goddess. He's projecting settled energy, cosy energy, caring energy. He's projecting, in fact, a desire for something exactly opposite to the energy he longs for: he's caught between two worlds, two opposing ideas of what might make a happy and fulfilled life. Vic is, we might surmise, a little troubled.

What is it that you want, Victor? How can you reconcile these two ways of being? That's a question for the Life Path, therapy and some big thinking – but by simply knowing that the tension exists, we open up new ways of understanding it. We understand that this tension exists within Vic, and that it may always exist. We understand that these two duelling aspects will inform his life going forward (and, perhaps, if they ever met – his relationship with Scarlett!).

4

CALCULATING YOUR LIFE PATH NUMBER

So if that's who we are, where must we go? Where will we walk? On the next few pages, we will learn to calculate the Life Path: the most crucial number in all Numerology. If you only have time for one, or want to simplify still further, this is the one to go for. This book is structured around the nine Life Paths – one for each digit. Within each Life Path are, of course, Personalities, but they are so much more than that. Each Life Path has its own challenges, and its own rewards. Each Life Path offers us a map, and a guide, to our possible goals and dreams – perhaps even dreams we don't know ourselves. We must come to our Life Path with an open mind: we must be open to finding new ways to go, and new people to become. We must be open to change, and new ideas. These Life Paths cannot tell our fortune. They cannot tell us, in fact, what to do at all. They can only tell us places we may go, and the places we will thrive. Open your heart; and open your mind; and allow yourself to thrive.

We add together the date of your birth, plus the number of the month of your birth, plus the year you were born.

It's pretty simple – but there's just one catch. We add each of those numbers separately – so if you were born on a double-digit day, you'll add both those digits together before you add the month. If you're born on the 17th, for example, that becomes 1 + 7, which makes 8.

Same goes for a month, if you're born in October, November or December: the 10th month becomes 1 + 0, meaning 1.

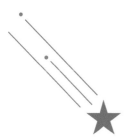

> **Each Life Path offers us a map, and a guide, to our possible goals and dreams.**

The 11th month becomes 1 + 1, which becomes 2. The 12th month becomes 1 + 2, which becomes 3.

Where it's most important is adding together the year. Obviously, years have four digits, and it's crucial to add each of those four digits together separately before we add it to the main number. The catch here is that you'll probably end up with a two-digit answer. Say you're born in 1989. You'll add 1 + 9 + 8 + 9, and wind up with 27: [2 + 7] = 9.

So, let's say your birthday is 17 October 1989: you'd wind up adding 8 (for 17) and 1 (for October's 1 + 0) and 9 (for 1989).

That comes to 18 and then we add those two digits together to give a Life Path number of 9.

You'll see two more examples on the opposite page, and space to work out your own number.

MARTHA

Martha's birthday is 7 August 1990 or 7/8/1990

[7] + [8] + [1 + 9 + 9 + 0]

7 + 8 + [19]

7 + 8 + [1+9]

7 + 8 + [10]

7 + 8 + [1+0]

7+8+1=16

1+6 = 7

Martha's Life Path is number 7: The Searcher

EDWIN

Edwin's birthday is 16 November 1977 or 16/11/1977

[1 + 6] + [1 + 1] + [1 + 9 + 7 + 7]

7 + 2 + [24]

7 + 2 + [2+4]

7 + 2 + 6 = 15

1 + 5 = 6

Edwin's Life Path is number 6: The Domestic Goddess

LIFE PATH ONE
THE MAGICIAN

Everything starts somewhere, and you, Number One, are where it all comes from. Without one, there can be no other; without one, there's nothing more. At this moment, everything is possible.

Picture the scene: a dark stage. Red velvet curtains, heavy, dusty. An audience, expectant. A single spotlight. And there – in the spotlight – you.

In one hand, your top hat. In the other, the deck of cards. The hush of the people, waiting to see what you'll do. Because you might do anything. A rabbit might appear from your hat, but what if it wasn't a rabbit? You might produce anything. You might do anything, or make anything happen. You're there in the centre stage, and you haven't done anything yet: it's all about what's about to happen, what's going to be. It's all about the moment that's next: the anticipation, the intake of breath. The single spotlight. The Magician breathes it in. The world is poised, watching the light. Then she opens her mouth, and then she speaks.

But hold it right there. That's you, Number One. You own that stage, and everyone watching. You own the moment – but admit it. You're

Well, hello there, sunshine. This is the beginning.

frustrated by that slow scene I just spun, because you want to know what happens next. You wanted to skip through the anticipation, and get right into it: to keep going, to make it happen, to watch it happen, and to be there when it does. You're thinking, I think, about the next beat: the next amazing thing you're about to do, the next amazing thing you're going to say. The thing that's going to set the world on fire.

But we know you're pure fire, flame emoji made flesh. Of course you are: you're the whole of the fire. You're both the spark and the whole vast sun. You're Leo, you're Apollo and Helios and Zeus. You're the lightbulb moment; the flick of a switch and the flash of a match. You're bright, and you're brilliant. You're a king.

And I say "king" advisedly. There's a certain kind of power, often associated with masculinity, that you carry with you. I don't mean butch, and I certainly don't mean to imply that it's only about or for men – but this Life Path has, historically, been imbued with powerful masculine energy. A swagger; a self-possession; a certain kind of confidence. A sense, sort of, of sexual power. You know what I mean, right? There's something of that in you: something as-yet untapped, maybe, or perhaps something in the way you're perceived that you don't yet recognize as your own. There's power here: real power, real energy, and you're going to use it. But let's not get too far ahead.

1

So...what about this moment? This still moment before it starts. This moment right now?

You can find this moment of stillness: it's within you.

You are the moment; and you are the beginning. So here's your first task, if you find yourself here: find the moment. I promise you, it's worth a try.

If you need them, there are guidelines below for an exercise that can help with this mindful possession of the moment. I know you're looking for something to do, something real, something that feels like momentum and mastery and success. The guidelines are there if you need them. But first, why not try it your own way? I promise you – not that you need promising – that you do know how

to do it. You pretty much know everything you need to know – and you know that, too, deep down. You can find this moment of stillness: it's within you. There's time in your busy life to pause.

THE FIVE SENSES
EXERCISE

When we want to be grounded in the moment, we need to be grounded in a sense of place, space and time. This exercise can be done anywhere, and takes just a few moments. It's about attention: about using our senses and thread of breath to pull us both into ourselves, and the place we're in right now.

We begin by sitting comfortably, perhaps cross legged, and starting to notice the breath. Don't change the breath: just observe. Is it deep? Is it shallow? Is it ragged? Try to watch it without deepening it – which is hard! It's hard not to try and "improve" what we perceive to be our failings. Observe the breath for at least 30 seconds: does it change? Is the inbreath as long as the outbreath? Longer? Shorter? Keep your attention on the breath as long as you can and, when you feel ready, turn that attention outward to your surroundings, and begin the exercise.

Look for:

- ♦ *Five things you can see*
- ♦ *Four things you can hear*
- ♦ *Three things you can feel*
- ♦ *Two things you can smell*
- ♦ *One thing you can taste*

And breathe. And breathe. And breathe.

Find the moment – this moment, with the book in your hands – that you're in right now. Because it's your moment.

Accept, here and now, at the beginning of the beginning: for you, there is only now.

Just: stop for a second. Right here, stop. Breathe in; breathe out: cool air in your mouth and throat and lungs. Feel the breath, and pause.

This is hard. It's always hard to stop – not in a minute, not in an hour, but now. There's always something else you could be doing; something you could be thinking about, striving for, making happen. There's always something that needs you more than this moment, and it's hard to pretend there isn't long enough to pause.

And maybe you aren't used to finding things hard; or maybe you're just not used to being allowed to admit it. If that resonates, sit with it.

What is it about admitting you're struggling that makes you uncomfortable? What is it that you feel about people who struggle – or people who stop? What is it you feel, maybe, about people who need help? Does it feel like weakness to need help? Does weakness frighten you? Sit with that, too.

The thing about being as sparky as you is that it can be hard to be patient with people who can't keep up. You might not show it, but it's frustrating as hell when you're trying to make something happen, and they can't see your vision.

Maybe they make it difficult for you to even articulate your vision – but you know it's there. You've got high standards, and strong convictions, and you know what you want. You know what you want, and you're pretty sure you know where you're going. Do you even need this guide at all? Do you need to follow anyone? You're a leader, not a follower...and yet, Number One, something brought you here. Something in you knows you're a little lost, even if you don't quite know where you went astray – and when you're a little lost, it's time to pause.

When you're a little lost, it's time to pause.

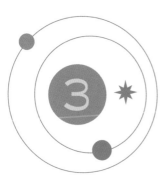

**You need
to recognise
your full and
mighty power,
and use it.**

9

So what's stopping you, Number One? What's holding you back on this journey? You're sparky. You're ambitious, too: you want to make things happen. You want to push for things to happen. So what's brought you here?

You know – even if it's only somewhere deep down – that you're just a little bit more special than people maybe think. You know you are; you know you're something extra. You know how good you are...don't you?

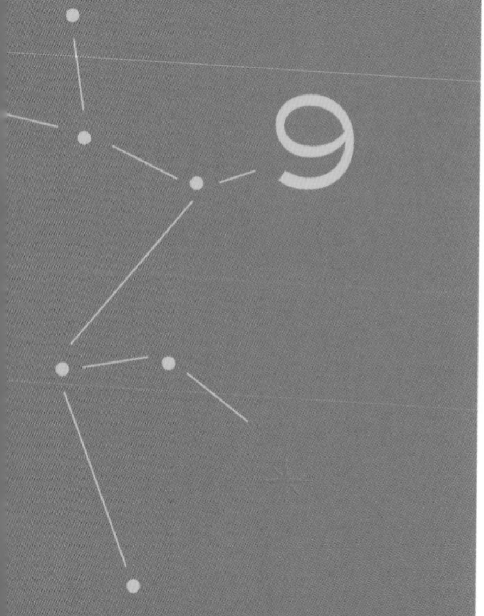

And perhaps this might be your second hurdle. No, not a hurdle, but a mission, a challenge: do you know how good you are?

Sit in that pause we just made and take a piece of paper. I want you to write down every single strength you have. Everything that you bring to a team, everything that you bring to the table. Don't be shy, here – we both know that shyness is stupid when it's just you, the paper and this page. If you've been suppressing this kind of feeling for a long time, you might struggle – but set that to one side. You know that's not you. You know you're more than this: you're charismatic, independent, driven, brave, generous, empathetic...You have a vision for what you want in life and, more than that, you have everything you need to achieve it. The sun is the start, and the sun is a star, and everyone who ever lived is stardust brought to life by the spark of the sun.

You have a powerful energy, Number One, and it's your duty to find out what it is. You can do something magical for the people around you – and for you, too. This is your mission, Magician. Your lifelong mission. A journey that starts today.

You need to recognize your full and mighty power, and use it.

LIFE PATH TWO
THE DREAMER

The Moon has many phases, and the Moon has many faces; and, Dreamer, I know you do, too.

Your Tarot card is the High Priestess; and your star signs are Gemini, the twins, and Virgo, the maiden; and Vulcan, the god of the fire and the forge, goes with you into the dark night. Janus, the two-faced god, looks over your future and your past, and sees all. And then Selene and Hecate, Artemis

and Luna, Juno and Hera: these are the goddesses, in all their guises, who belong to the Moon one way or another. But then, who doesn't?

The Moon, you see, pulls the tide. And there is a tide in everything – not just in the affairs of men, as Shakespeare said, and not just in the ocean – but in a very real, physical sense. We are mostly made, quite literally, of water. Salt water. Each of us carries around a great aquarium of salts and fluids within us, perfect oceans calibrated to carry everything we are, and everything we can be. And those individual tiny oceans are pulled by the Moon, too.

It's a recognized phenomenon that hospital emergency departments are busier and more chaotic at a full Moon. The police, speaking anecdotally, also recognize the Full Moon Effect – and any person who has ever had a menstrual period understands the cyclical hormonal tug of the wax and wane.

The Moon pulls the tides; and the Moon changes everything; and the Moon, herself, is constantly changing. But there is a rhythm to her changes: there is a cycle, and a pattern that may be observed.

This is the Life Path of the Dreamer. The way is shaped by our creative subconscious, and perhaps we sometimes feel out of control: as if we don't fully understand the choices we're making, the changes that are happening. The dreamer sleeps, but the dream rolls on. Are we in control, or is something else pulling us? Is something else pushing us? How can we better understand ourselves to feel more in control?

Every great dream begins with a dreamer.

2

DREAM JOURNAL

You may have preconceptions about the words "dream journal", but stick with me: I promise it has both spiritual and practical worth. To understand our creative subconscious we have to get to know it: we have to get to know ourselves.

You see, according to Jungian theory, we play every character in our dreams. Everyone you see while you sleep is your own impression of that person: not your mother, for instance, but all your ideas about your mother rolled into one, and given voice by you – like an actor with a puppet. When we dream of a person, it doesn't tell us what that person really is, but it can tell us more about our ideas of that person. The same is true, of course, for places; places, people, objects and actions. Noticing our dreams – and considering them – can tell us what we're dwelling on; and give us insight into our deepest and most secret mind.

So let's grab a notebook and pen. That's the first bit of this exercise.

Set them by your bed. That's the second part.

You can figure out the third part, right? Sadly, this is not the kind of exercise you do once and move on; this is a lifetime's work. Just like understanding your Life Path. Every morning, the first thing you do when you wake up – I want you to take a deep breath in, grab your pen and paper, and on the exhale – jot down what you can remember about your dreams.

Here's the catch: I want you to do this in just three words. I want you to breathe, and I want you to write three words only.

There are, of course, a lot of benefits to writing a longer journal. But in this one, we're trying for something a little different. What we're going for is consistency: we're going for easy, we're going for reliable. We're going for the idea that you can make this happen every day, in a way that makes sense for you, no matter what other demands there are on your time.

Before you do anything else, commune with your own mind. Communicate with the deep self and listen to what she has to say. Take time for yourself. Take time for the Moon.

Over time, you will build up a bank of images and motifs that have been preoccupying your mind. You'll start to see patterns. You'll start to see cycles – and when you see cycles, you can better understand how to lean into them, or break them. You'll see them change, and perhaps even learn to move better with them: the tide of yourself, the Moon that pulls your dreams.

Dreamer, you're more sensitive to hurt than maybe others seem, whether you let on or not. You feel things deeply and perhaps privately. Does that make you avoid confrontation? Does that make you afraid? Think now, perhaps, of your own power.

The Moon is powerful. Hera was the wife of Zeus, and Artemis the twin sister of Apollo. This Life Path is marked by equal power to the Magician; and yet it's a different power, a subtler kind of power. The power of a light in the darkness. The power of the pull of the waves; the power of a nurse on a late shift; of maiden, mother, and wise woman.

It's not that this path, the Dreamer's path, is only for women, in the same way that the path of the Magician might be walked by anyone of any gender. But we have to be real: there is a powerful femininity to this way, an energy that lifts and uplifts the female experience in every changeable, shifting form. There's a softness, a strength; a certain indefinable tender femme slant to this

You feel things deeply and perhaps privately.

7

Moon-tinged dreamscape that we can't ignore.

Let's take a moment here, and pause to wonder: what does this mean to you? How does this sit with you? Might this, in and of itself, be part of your challenge? Let's stay with this for a moment: what does that femininity look like in your life? In your mind? How could we make that understanding richer, wider, stronger?

We're lucky we no longer live in an age when our lives are circumscribed by the fact of our femaleness; we're lucky, most of us, to live in a time and place where gender is not the be-all and end-all of our ambition and scope for life. And yet it's true, still, that we can't escape gender. Much like numbers and language, gender is a construct

– and yet like them, too, the roots go deep. Deep, and thirsty. Gender pulls at us like the current in a river, like hands shaping clay – we can't avoid it, no matter how hard we try, and that means we carry with us both the consequences and the connotations of who we were born, and who we are now. Sit, now, and use this moment to ask yourself: how do I feel about femininity? How do I feel about accepting that femininity as part of me? How do I feel about embracing that? This goes double if you've come to this Life Path from a more traditionally masculine mindset: if anything, for you, this question is only more urgent, and more compelling.

How we embrace strength, how we accept tenderness and how we greet change: these are the challenges of your life, and they will take a lifetime to perfect.

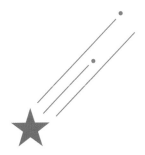

LIFE PATH THREE
THE STORYTELLER

Three's the charm. Third time lucky. Three wishes, three bears and three kings following a star. The holy trinity. Maiden, mother and crone. There's a natural rhythm to story beats and sentence fragments arriving in three parts: think of the beginning, the middle and the end. For three, you see, is the number of the storyteller.

And that, Number Three, is you.

I don't know how that manifests in your life, or whether this is a gift you're going to work at and develop, but I know that within you is a storyteller. There's magic there: you have a creative, sparky genius that you can harness to take you wherever you want to go. People listen to you. They admire you. They respect you, because the person who controls the narrative controls everything else, too. When did you learn that? How young were you when you realized that if you could just somehow get ahead of what the others were thinking – say it yourself, maybe, or even say something about someone else – you could skip out on suffering? How long have you been trying to tell the story so that someone else won't tell it for you?

Those who tell the stories rule the world.

And let's be real: you're not wrong. There's nothing wrong with what you're doing; and nothing wrong with being the one who does it. For Mercury is the ruler of the astrological third house, and Mercury is the messenger of the gods. You, too, are a messenger. You have something to say, and your life's work is going to be learning how to say it.

And maybe this seems kind of... simple to you? Not really a "life's work" at all. Maybe you think you're a straight-talking sort of person: say what you mean, and mean what you say.

3

But if that's the case, what are you missing? And what could you hear if you stopped talking? Storyteller, a key task for you is to learn to listen. And listen, too, without judgement. When you meet someone, what might it feel like to accept them on their terms? What might it feel like to accept their story, instead of yours – or even to weave both stories together? How much richer might your stories be if you incorporated the stories and lives of others – or if you gave a voice to those who find themselves voiceless? In your quest to tell your story, who have you not heard?

See, maybe you already know what story you're going to tell, and maybe you're just going to open your mouth and get it out into the world. Maybe you've already started spinning this yarn, and

It is rare to be loved for who you really are, and your original, beautiful mind deserves that.

maybe you've already got people listening. Maybe they already love you. And this we know to be true, Storyteller: you have the capacity to inspire people; to drive them; to make them sit and listen. You make communities. You make societies. You make spaces with your stories, and people love you for it. Three is the number of friendship, traditionally – think of the Tarot card Three of Cups – and you are loved. You have the capacity to be deeply loved – and more than that, loved for yourself. It is rare to be loved for who you really are, and your original, beautiful mind deserves and craves that. But do you feel loved, Storyteller? Really loved?

The thing is, in all this sparkle and spin, do you ever wonder if something has been lost?

No, don't worry. Don't panic. I won't tell anyone; and nobody knows: your quiet moments, those flickers of fear, are yours alone. Everyone else thinks spinning all these plates is easy for you, and it's not always. You keep up appearances beautifully. You never let on. The guilt, the shame, the stress – that's not part of the story.

Dazzle has a price, and you pay it gladly. But the ease with which you hand over the toll doesn't mean it's free. That's something you have to reckon with, and will have to reckon with all your life: is this worth it? Is this act of creativity worth what I'm giving to make it? And I don't just mean creativity in a traditional artsy sense: I mean creative thinking, creative domesticity, creative living. Where will the payment come from? What well will you draw from to tell this story, to live this story?

Your Tarot card is The Empress: the fertile, creative, beautiful Empress. If you look at the Tarot card for The Empress, number III, you'll see fields of golden wheat and lush green grasses and a burbling winding stream. You live with abundance, or should live with abundance. Do you feel that abundance in your life? That might be in material things; it might be in ideas. It might even be in people. It might be in your hopes, and everything you hope to spin into reality: the Storyteller is kind of like a mama spider in the centre of a beautiful silken web, waiting and making and waiting and making and spinning the story into something world changing. And like the spider, you are in abundance – whether you know it or not. Give yourself a little space now to think about abundance.

You are in abundance, whether you know it or not.

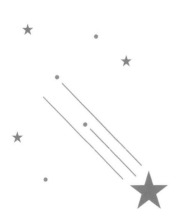

9

BEGIN YOUR STORY

Take a pen and paper: we're going to make not just a story, but a real, tangible thing you can pin on the wall or stick to the fridge.

Right here, right now, make a list. Make a real list of the things you have that make you feel great: that make you feel lucky and rich and happy.

A cup of tea in the morning. A phone call with your best friend. A bubble bath. The idea you have for a novel that you haven't written yet. Keep writing. Keep writing until the page is full. Dig deep and dig thorough.

Where are you most rich? Where are you most fertile, and most creative?

This is the place where your work begins, Storyteller. Nobody can grow without being planted in a rich soil, and this list will be something we can come back to when times get tough.

For times will get tough. Not even the magic of narrative can keep away pain or charm back grief: these things will come for you, as they come for us all. So, Storyteller, some questions for you: how would you tell a story where you do not come out on top? And how would you tell a story if you could not find the words? Where might you find the words? Where might you find strength? What kind of stories can you tell without words? What kind of stories can you tell when the ending is written for you? When you're the loser? When you're the villain? We think about these questions now so that when these things happen, you're still the best person you know you can be...and that your story is still your own. You're magical, Storyteller. You're the person running the show. But

don't forget that you're a person, too. You're a person with needs, and wants, and desires, and flaws, and problems, and love. You're not just the narrator, and you're not just a character. For life isn't always story shaped. You break things off. You lose things. You embellish others. You shape it and make it and work at it.

What would the truth feel like, if you told it?

Would it feel like – could it feel like – breathing out?

LIFE PATH FOUR
THE MASTER

What does the word "masterpiece" mean to you?

It's come to mean something basically flawless: something that only the most gifted and special of artists might make once in a lifetime. Something outstanding. Something out of reach of almost everyone. An idea, basically, that almost everything will fail to meet.

And yet, it used to mean something subtly and profoundly different.

In the workshops of Old Europe, hundreds of years ago, it meant not an idea but an object.

A series of objects, in fact: one for each master of each craft.

For a master of a craft was a person, pure and simple, who had produced a masterpiece; and in producing the masterpiece had transitioned from apprentice to a permanent member of the guild.

An apprentice was a young person learning from the greats, and learning the ways of a craft: a young person with a dream to make something, not just for themselves, but for the world. They were learning to make beautiful things; and to be recognized for making beautiful things, and the first piece that really mattered was the masterpiece. The masterpiece was a gift, of sorts, to the guild: to the greats who came before them, and the humble hopefuls who would come after. In artists' workshops and goldsmiths' studios, in the rooms of leather-workers and knife-makers and sugar-spinners, in all the places where things were made and things were done: there were beginners striving to be the best they could be.

The great and glorious masterpiece of humanity is to know how to live with a purpose.

4

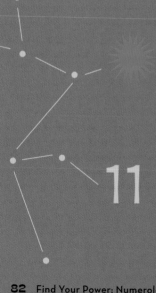

And when the masterpiece was done? That didn't mark the end of the work. It marked the beginning.

I've always liked looking at the word this way, because of what it tells us about the real nature of success: about being recognized by your peers, about being inspired and inspiring, about striving upward and onward and toward something bigger and better and more beautiful. I think you will, too, Four. Your Tarot card is The Emperor: big, masculine energy, with a zeal and zest for work and growth that puts others to shame. (And it does put others to shame

– but we'll get to that.) Does this resonate with you? It might – but maybe not.

Think of the story of the apprentice, and the way the masterpiece meant only the beginning of yet more work and study and care. The masterpiece was – in some senses – just a waymarker on their quest, and maybe you understand that all too deeply. Do you even notice when you've achieved the thing you were working toward? Or do you just keep charging on to the next thing? Do you stop and smell the roses in the garden you've planted, or do you start thinking about how you should paint the fences and sweep the yard?

I have a friend who each year, in place of New Year's Resolutions, makes a list of Last Year's Achievements. It helps her feel grounded, and safe. Four, I think you need to feel grounded and safe to achieve everything you must achieve. I think you need to take stock of everything that got you here.

SELF-ESTEEM JOURNAL

Let's make a list of your accomplishments: of everything that got you here, and everything you've achieved so far. Seem impossible? Get used to it. You're the Master, and your life is about making the impossible seem not just possible, but easy. Through work, rigorous discipline and really, truly loving what you do, you turn chaos into something orderly. And not just orderly, but beautiful.

And that beauty, Master, starts with you. You need to recognize everything you've done that brought you to this point: every success, every milestone. Every masterpiece. I'm not going to give directions for your Accomplishment List – though I urge you to do it in real life, on the front pages of a new notebook. Because from now on, I want you to check in with yourself in this notebook at the start of every day.

Every day, I'd like you to jot something down for these six categories:

- *Something you did for your physical health*

- *Something you did for your mental health*

- *Something you did for someone else*

- *Something that made you happy*

- *Something you achieved*

- *Something you hope to achieve tomorrow*

I want you to notice your accomplishments. I want you to recognize how hard you work, and the results that come from that. You're the boss; a powerful, creative, disciplined force for good in the world. And you deserve to feel that way.

Slow down for a minute, Four. Your forward march to success is brilliant, but it can be brutal, too. You go and you go and you go, but here with this book in your hands, you can take a moment – and I think you know you need a moment – to breathe.

Give yourself space to think about what you've done. And the thing is, this gives other people space to see it, too. They need space, and they need time. You love what you do, and you want others to love what you do, too. In fact, you can't understand why anyone does anything they don't love – or why they can't just make themselves love it. When you have a task to do, you just...get on with it. Why can't other people do the same? You don't like fuss, and you don't like faff. You don't like excuses, either. It makes you feel like things aren't safe when people don't know what they're doing. Uncertainty makes you feel like there are unnecessary risks. Your foundation is unshakeable, deep down – but you don't like incompetence, and

you don't like dithering. Your belief in yourself is everything, and it's justified. You are the person you most hope you can be. And you hold other people to those same exacting, rigid standards.

Your belief in yourself is everything, and it is justified.

9

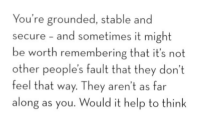

You're grounded, stable and secure – and sometimes it might be worth remembering that it's not other people's fault that they don't feel that way. They aren't as far along as you. Would it help to think

If you want to be a master, you have to learn to reach out.

of them as the apprentice? They are learning, and they will learn from you.

You understand the rules we're all supposed to be playing by. Actually, you probably helped write them. Give them space; give them guidance. Your challenge here is to learn to lead: to be a leader, an emperor. You have kingship written in your stars. This is part of your purpose here on Earth, and everyone's life's work is to learn their purpose and carry it out.

If you want to be a master – and I know that you do – you have to learn to reach out to those coming up behind you. You have to learn to teach not only yourself, but also people less capable, less clever, less practical than yourself. You have to have patience.

Patience, and tenderness. That's not faff. Don't ignore this message. You deserve these things, regardless of your work, regardless of success.

This is the universe speaking. Your ruling planet, Uranus, is one not just of the forward march of revolution, but of renewal. You must make time to renew, and for that you need love. You need kindness. You need time, and you need tenderness.

Make time for tenderness, Four. You are not your job. You are not, in fact, any one thing at all. You are everything you think you are, and more. So much more. Let yourself just be.

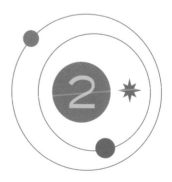

LIFE PATH FIVE
THE FREE SPIRIT

Here's a place for you to imagine when things get hard: picture a waterfall. A vast waterfall, tumbling and powerful, thundering down into a fathomless icy pool, and then meandering on to the next fall, twisting and turning, a kink here, an eddy there. The mountains around rise purple and mighty, and the sky goes on forever. Maybe stars. Maybe sunset. Maybe sunrise. And you, standing on the precipice of the waterfall – and a skinny-dip swan-dive down into the sparkling depths. And come up smiling.

And see, Free Spirit, where the river takes you.

This is your place: ultimate freedom, independence from everything, and a flexible, powerful control over your own body. You crave this: you need it. You need life to be an adventure, and when you feel trapped you feel – somehow – lost. Here, in the heart of the wilderness, you know exactly who you are. I want you, now, to imagine this happy place. Embellish it. Tweak it. But the waterfall, and the river before and beyond it: keep those.

A free spirit takes liberties even with liberty itself.

That river is life, Free Spirit, ever onward and ever changing. The waterfalls and kinks and twists and turns are everything life throws at us. But you knew that. You know about change, and the inevitability of change. You know how life can surprise you: will always surprise you. Is that scary? Of course it's scary. But it's exciting, too. And learning to balance that – the fear and the joy – is your life's work. Your path is not an easy one, Free Spirit. Your path is the path of change. Of course, all paths lead to change somehow – but for you? For you, above all, you have to embrace this change.

You have to not fight it. You have to learn to love it. This is the primary challenge of your path, and it won't be easy.

We get stuck in patterns so easily in our lives, often without even thinking about it. We follow old grooves of thinking. Don't believe me? You inhabit a very physical realm, so let's try a really physical example. Fold your arms. Fine. Normal. Now...fold them the other way, with the other arm on top. It feels weird to swap them, right? Can you even do it? See, there's no reason you should fold your arms one way or another, but you always do it that same way. You've got a pattern, and it's hard to break out of it.

Now, with folded arms it doesn't make much difference – but what about everything else in your life that's stuck one way, and you haven't even noticed? The thing is, you wouldn't be here, reading this book, if you weren't looking for something a little different. You know something needs to change, and you know something is stuck. And are you, perhaps, a little afraid? That's not the kind of thing you love to admit. What does it feel like to admit it?

You have to not fight change. You have to learn to love it.

EMBRACE TERROR, CHANGE AND POWER

Here's an idea: today, I want you to do something that scares you. A little thing. A big thing. One scary thing.

I'm not going to give you an example of what counts as big or what counts as small: it varies for all of us. For me, it's easy to speak in front of 300 strangers, but it's almost impossible to open a letter from the bank. For you, you might be brilliant at that kind of admin, but paralysed at the thought of telling someone how you really feel. For your friend, she might be brilliant at articulating her emotions, but become incredibly stressed at the prospect of cycling home instead of taking the bus.

Here's what I want you to think about when you do this:

♦ *How did you feel before?*

♦ *How did you feel during?*

♦ *How did you feel after?*

Free Spirit, your life is not supposed to be constrained by fear. Your life is supposed to be one of change, of explorations, of gambles. Use this framework as your prompt – and repeat. Live bigger. Live braver.

Your associated Tarot card is The Hierophant. Unlike other Tarot cards, the name of this one doesn't give much away to the modern reader – and many readings of the card imply a reliance on structures like the Church. The Hierophant

Five is a very spiritual number and you are a deeply spiritual person.

is sometimes called the Pope, and he's the masculine counterpart to The High Priestess (see page 64): he's a spiritual teacher, a learned man, someone who respects family and institutions. Which kind of

seems like the exact opposite of your Free Spirit path, right? What's the Church if not a series of patterns and traditions. Exactly the kind of thing that makes you feel trapped! So what gives?

Let's look first at the big picture of the card: what's this guy doing? What's the point of a Hierophant, or a Pope? Well, he's got a mission. He's got something to do: a deep, spiritual, practical purpose on this Earth. He's not just a CEO, and he's not some monk. He's a person who marries the conscious with the subconscious, the dream with the day. He's the person who translates humanity's beautiful drifts of faith into something real. You can learn from this, Free Spirit. You're not meant to live a mundane life.

You're there, ready to take your life in your own two hands and dive in.

10

Five is a very spiritual number – the Five Pillars of Islam, the Five Precepts of Buddhism, the Five Wise Virgins of the Bible – and you are a deeply spiritual person. And yet, somehow, you're also the sensual five-fingers, five-toes, five-senses skinny dipper. You're a practical person with a zest for living, and you need a purpose that marries those two things. You need a quest.

So let's call that your second challenge: you need to find a purpose. What motivates you, Free Spirit? What spurs you on? What do you wish you could tell other people? What do you wish you could give them? How can you share your freedom with others who need it, too? Can you ever achieve the freedom you need while other people labour in chains? How can you direct your extraordinary energy and capacity toward others? What can you usefully do?

Look: The Hierophant has two hands, and with one he points to the sky, and with the other to the Earth. He holds himself between the spiritual and the physical; between the need to fly away, and the deep need to stay grounded. You don't do well if you let either half of yourself win too much ground, Free Spirit. You need to stay in the here and now, but you also need sparkle, and spiritual magic. The Hierophant tells us that your last task is balance. Remember that waterfall? That's the world, ever changing, and you – on the precipice – must be perfectly balanced.

The idea of accidents scares you. You love control, and you love to have control over your own body and your own destiny above everything else. So how to find balance? The waterfall rushes on. The river snakes forever forward. And you're there, poised, ready to take your life in your own two hands and dive. Dive, and swim forward into the future: the current and the kick and pull of your own true strong self, working together.

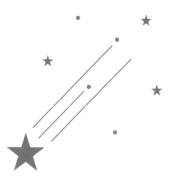

LIFE PATH SIX
THE DOMESTIC GODDESS

Venus and Virgo, Gaia and your Tarot card The Lovers: yours, Goddess, is the path of empathy and compassion. You walk in the world as a force for harmony and stability; for love, awareness and peace.

Don't be put off by the term "Goddess", please, if you're starting from a more masculine

place – and try not to mind the powerful feminine energy of Virgo and Venus and Gaia either. These energies have been associated for millennia with women and girls. While, one hopes, we're moving past that into a more enlightened society now, we can't escape the forces and ideas that have shaped us into who we are. The Life Path of Six is essentially a life path of homemaking: not in the ironing and mopping sense, but in the creative, radical act of building a life worth having. Not just that: a life worth having where we are.

The Life Path of the Domestic Goddess is accepting the life you have, and building on it to make it into something beautiful. It's about knowing that everyone needs a home; and everyone needs somewhere to feel safe; and knowing that you have it in you to make that happen.

You need quiet, Goddess, but the quiet of a well-run home rather than the depths of the wild forest. Give me a lever and a steady place to stand, said Archimedes, and I will move the world. You, Goddess, both create and crave that steady place.

Change frightens you. Change unsettles you – and when you're unsettled, you're uneasy and spiky and sad. You spook like a thoroughbred horse, when things seem uncertain – and oh, you're so certain about some things. You're sure you know exactly how to make things right; and you're sure your way is the right way. You give the best advice – or, at least, you think you do. So why don't people follow it? If everyone would just do it your way, you could keep them safe. You could make everything nice. It

Home is where the heart is.

6

could be so nice, if only they would do your thing and not their own.

The thing about you, Goddess, is that you have a deep well of creativity in you: the kind of powerful, beautiful creativity that leads people to write novels and embroider tapestries and direct full-length epic movies. You have to harness that creativity somehow. Let loose, you turn it on the people around you, and wonder why they don't do exactly as you might wish. This is frustrating for everyone! You hate it, and so do they! You're not a control freak: you just can't bear the idea that anyone you love might get less than their due. Only you can give them their due, right! Only you can do justice to their story! Surely, this is all your responsibility? Well, no. Come on, Goddess. You have to let people live their own way.

So here's your first challenge: you need to foster and find an outlet for your creativity.

This might be taking up knitting. This might be cooking, or gardening or another aspect of the deep creativity of happy domesticity. But then again, Goddess, it might be something completely out of your comfort zone. Write. Paint. Join a choir. Draw. Whatever it is, I'd like you to try to do it regularly. Spend that time with yourself, in your own body and mind. When did you last take time just for you?

THE 30 CIRCLES EXERCISE

Here's an exercise that is a great place to start forcing yourself to accept and encourage your creativity – and to take it to a healthier outlet. This task is in three parts.

For your first exercise, take a sheet of paper and a pen. On the paper, I'd like you to draw 30 circles. Yes, you heard me right. Thirty circles. Some big, some small. Fill the paper with your 30 circles. Now, your reaction to this challenge will be interesting, too. Do you feel silly? When was the last time you drew anything? Why 30? Do you feel like you're wasting time? Notice how you feel. Notice, too, how you feel when the circles aren't perfect! Did you wonder if you should be drawing round something, like a mug? Did you maybe even use a compass? Perfectionist Virgo is watching over you, and she gets it.

Ready for the second part? You'll need six minutes, and a timer to count them off on. In these six minutes, I want you to draw something in each of those thirty circles. You heard me: in each of those 30 circles, I want you to draw something. No, it won't be perfect. Yes, some will be better than others. No, you don't have enough time! But you're drawing, aren't you? You're doing it! Go! Notice how you feel: notice whether you feel exhilarated, frightened, stressed, silly, happy or rushed. Notice which drawings you feel good about. I don't care if you can't draw. Not the point. The point is to make something: the point is to foster a creativity that comes all from you.

And then, the hard part. Over the next 30 days, I want you to pick one of these circles every single day. I want you to pick a circle, and write something about that circle:

what you drew, what it might mean, what it could be. How you felt. How it makes you feel. How you feel about being asked to do this exercise. I suggest doing this first thing in the morning, with a cup of tea, or the moment you sit down at your desk, or last thing at night. Make it a little routine for the 30 days to sit down with your own creativity, and build on it. You don't have to write much – just a couple of sentences. Just enough to find a spark. Just enough to warm yourself up, or sing yourself to sleep.

How do you feel at the end of the 30 days? Did this routine help? Did you feel more creative? If so, do it again. You might switch it up this time: write a word in each circle, and every day use the words as a prompt. A colour in each circle that prompts another drawing, each day for 30 days. Be your own guide; your own teacher. Sit with yourself. Love yourself.

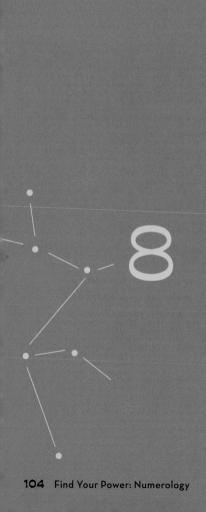

The thing is, Goddess, in all your working to make home nice for others, how much time do you spend looking after yourself? Carve out a space that belongs only to you, or risk resenting others for not doing it for you. Your Tarot card is The Lovers, and The Lovers is the card of compromise: of shared lives, of equality, of balance. Of soft, easy living that takes into equal account your needs, and the needs of another. Of many others, perhaps, although don't spread yourself too thin. Your needs matter, too.

And maybe we're starting from a scarcity principle: how often does someone help you? How often do your needs get met by someone else? But then again, how often do you ask? You make it look so easy that perhaps others may be intimidated, or simply not know what to say. You live this life as the mama of the house, controlling and praising and judging – what might life be like if you saw other people as your equals? What if you saw the risks they take not as a threat to your collective safety, but as a step forward into the collective unknown?

You see, life doesn't punish, Goddess. Consequences are not the same thing as punishments. You get to feel free if you want to. You get to work toward freedom; you get to make choices; you get to do what you want. And so does everyone else.

You don't need to mete out justice, or cajole with rewards. You don't have to be anybody's saviour; and nobody has to save you. You are not responsible for the soul of anyone else – only your own. Your choices are all you can control. For everything else – for everyone else – the universe will provide.

LIFE PATH SEVEN
THE SEARCHER

If I said to you that seven is a magic number, would you roll your eyes?

You are perhaps too polite for that, but you might think it.

Lucky number seven stands for the seven sins, seven wonders and seven days a week; and there's a little part of your mind, even now in a book on numerology, that wants to tell me that that means nothing. A little part of your mind that

doubts all of this; or, conversely, a little part of your mind that wants to believe. Yours is a true journey, Searcher: a journey to reconcile the broken parts of yourself into one. Your Tarot card is The Chariot, and truly you have far to go. You will travel the distance between what you know and what you believe; between your head and your heart; your conscious mind and your unconscious gut. Yours is the philosopher's path; the problem-solver's way. It's a lonely way, to be sure. But what you find at the end will be worth it: for your quest is for nothing more, or less, than the truth.

You want the truth about the universe. You want big answers for big questions; and you want your need for the truth to be respected. You hate to be patronized and looked down on. In fact, you hate to look up to anybody. You need to be seen and respected as an equal by everyone: you're not a child. You won't be patronized with glib fairy tales. You need to know the truth about the universe.

You know what it is you want to know, and you're pretty sure about that: you know the kind of thing you want to find, and perhaps you even have an idea of what the truth is going to be when you find it. Wait a minute, though: when was the last time you changed your mind? Have you ever changed your mind?

It can be hard to be so rigid in what you long for, and when you're going on a lengthy journey you need to invite a little flexibility, and a little empathy, along for the ride. You're not better than the world around

May the road rise up to meet you, and the wind be always at your back.

7

you: don't let your pride tell you that. Don't be a snob! You're part of this beautiful world – yes, you, with your fierce critical thinking and unusual soul. You belong here, and accepting that you belong is part of your journey, too.

Searcher, I don't want to tell you how hard this path is. And I don't have to tell you. You know already, with the clarity and brilliance of a diamond, how difficult it can be to speak your truth or to hear that of another.

You're linked to Helios, driving his sun-chariot across the sky – but this also calls to mind Icarus: the boy who flew too close to the sun, and fell. You are not the bright light of truth yourself, but you crave it. You need it. You're the kind of person, perhaps, who as a kid pushed her finger through the soft flame of a candle, back and forth, back and forth. You remember that? How you couldn't believe how gentle it was? How it was only air, when you could see the light? And then, perhaps, how you moved your finger just a little too fast through the gentle golden part, and caught the real leaping blue triangle of heat beneath? And you remember, I suspect, the pain.

Still, the pain was interesting, wasn't it? It was something new to know. And for you, it's always been about knowledge. There's something of the solitary sage about you, Searcher: something of the lonely, or even aloof. You might hide it well, but there's part of you that always feels just a little detached. When you hurt, does it ever feel like there's a small bit of your mind that's thinking: huh, interesting? When you suffer, do you ever notice yourself kind of... analysing why? This part of you so badly wants to keep you safe that it detaches: your defence mechanisms run deep, and nothing is more destructive to a defence mechanism than going all in on something. Especially if that something is an emotion.

When was the last time you went all in on an emotion, Searcher? When was the last time you let yourself feel your feelings? What would happen if you did?

THE FEELINGS WHEEL

The diagram opposite is something called the Feelings Wheel. Two versions were simultaneously developed by two separate psychologists, Gloria Willcox and Robert Plutchik, in the Eighties, and it is a tool to help us name what we're going through. See, the wheel is really constructed of three wheels: an inner wheel, a central wheel and an outer wheel.

The inner wheel is labelled with the basic emotions. Willcox had these as mad, sad, scared, joyful, powerful and peaceful. Plutchik had them as joy, sadness, acceptance, disgust, fear, anger, surprise and anticipation. Six for Willcox, and eight for Plutchik, averages out to seven for us – and doesn't that feel kind of meant to be, Searcher? You can be sceptical, but I know a sign when I see one. We're going to use Willcox's wheel here, because it's better tailored to a non-expert working at home – but feel free to look up both.

Then, the outer wheels show further divisions of these emotions into the specifics: "scared", for instance, leads to rejected, confused, helpless; rejected plus confused leads to bewildered, discouraged and insignificant.

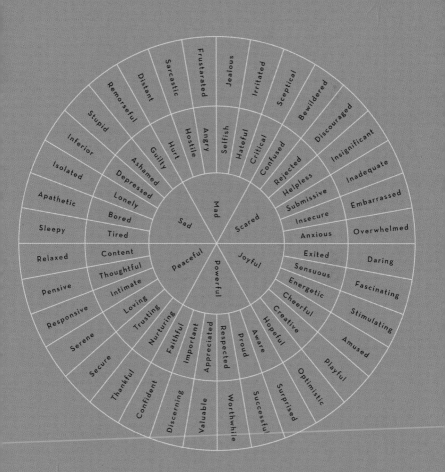

You know what I'm going to ask you to do here, Searcher
– and it is, in its own way, a search for a different kind of
knowledge. I'm going to ask you to consider, every day for
a seven-day week, the truth about yourself. I'd like you to
set a reminder on your phone: two reminders, one in the
morning and one at lunchtime; and I'd like you to open
a document or take a fresh page in your notebook, and
make a little chart. Give yourself plenty of room. Label the
columns "AM" and "PM"; label the rows with the days of the
week. Every day, twice a day, I want you to come back to
this wheel and check in with your emotions.

At the end of the week, consider: are there patterns?
Do you see anything different? Do you see anything that
surprises you? Turn your beautiful analytical mind inward,
and solve the puzzle that is you.

You need to feel, Searcher. You need to feel not only what the world is, but who you are in it.

Sometimes you have instinctively retreated from the world in order to better understand it, and the plain truth is that it's not going to get you there. You need to be in it, Searcher. You need to get your hands dirty. You need to get stuck in.

LIFE PATH EIGHT
THE DRAGON

This Life Path is so powerful, so lucky, that there have been cases of people changing their names to take on an Eight Life Path. It's the Life Path of power: of financial power, above all, of wealth and money and control and abundance. It's the power of stubborn instinct and careful choices and flashes of brilliant insight. You rise to every challenge; can face down every fear. It's the most seductive of journeys: the material girl, the arm loads of

jewels and bulging wallets and, dragon-like, hoards of gold.

I call this Life Path the Dragon because of all the gold. Well, sort of. Take the Dragon as your emblem, here, Eight: a lucky Chinese dragon, or a traditional Western jewel thief just as you please. The might of the Dragon is yours. The wealth of the Dragon is yours. And the flaws of the Dragon are your flaws, and the ones you must most carefully guard against.

The Tarot card numbered eight is sometimes Justice; but in other decks the number eight might be rendered as Strength. Justice is, of course, depicted as a judge with great scales of gold: she means fairness, integrity, balance and, above all, cause and effect. In her other hand she carries a sword.

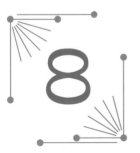

The rule of law; the rule of power, the rule of blood. Strength is a maiden riding a lion: the mighty and the sweet, the hunter tamed, the monster softened; and the bravery of the pure at heart. The same patterns recur, you see, in these two cards: they are all about the delicate line that must be walked between brute strength and great power; and softness, tenderness and mercy.

Your job in this life is to keep both in mind. As Justice sits with her scales, so you must find balance between the two.

Your power is of the mind: you are driven, quick and goal-oriented. You know what you want, and you know how to get it. You are capable of putting mind over matter (a young girl riding the great lion), and your rewards will come in time. You will invest in yourself, over and over again. You would – or should – bet on yourself, every time. You have everything you need, and you know it. Do you know it?

An adventure isn't worth telling if there aren't any dragons in it.

AFFIRMATIONS CHALLENGE

Dragon, you know that nobody else is going to believe in you if you don't. You're both the bookie and the horse, here: you have to be at peak performance, but you also have to put the money in. You have to put in the money – metaphorically speaking. You're what you can count on, and you have to believe it's true.

I'd like you to write three affirmations: three powerful invocations of your own strength and greatness. Don't worry, you don't need to tell them to anyone else – in fact, I'd advise keeping them to yourself if you want people to like you! Consider:

I am strong. I am brave. I am powerful.

or

I value myself. I value my opinions. I value my mind.

or

I can do this. I can do this. I can do this.

I want you to say this to yourself every morning, in the mirror. Wash your face, brush your teeth and tell yourself the truth: you are brave, you are strong, you are loved. Whatever you need to hear, hear it from yourself first. Studies have shown that this kind of self-talk is incredibly valuable: that when we tell ourselves we are brave, we become brave. We become the dragon we have to be to get the job done. We become mighty; we become capable. We become whoever we want to be. We manifest our own joy, and our own strength.

You have to be the person you know you can be.

You have to be the person you know you can be; and you have to know it. If you don't know it, how will anyone else? Your power comes from within: it's internal, not external. It's your self-belief and drive that will get you where you're going. Manifesting is your greatest talent: you wish, you work, and so it is so. You have a Midas touch, in the best way possible. You have the rare power of being able to imagine a plan from start to finish, and having the will to execute your whim to perfection. Love this about yourself, Dragon. Love the power within you. Don't be ashamed; don't hide your light under a bushel. You can't, anyway: people will notice. People notice

how extraordinary you are. Shine out, and be brave, and let people love you for who you are.

You love them, of course. You love them with a loyalty and strength that few can match; you will defend your loved ones to the end of time. You provide for them like nobody else. That's love, to you: to look after them, to keep them safe, to bring them home everything they've ever wanted.

But could it be more? Could you let tenderness into your life? Love is more complicated than money, sure – but you're brilliant, Dragon, in all ways. So why hold back when it comes to your heart?

The sword and the lion's sharp teeth show us you can be ruthless, Dragon: you can be brisk and curt, no hearts and flowers here. You like things done, and you like things done right. You can be manipulative and cruel, even, to get what you want. You're the ultimate provider for the people you love, but heaven help anyone who crosses you. In fact, heaven help anyone who gets in your way – accidentally or on purpose. Can you practise tenderness today?

A lack of understanding of your own vulnerability leaves you more vulnerable. If you don't know yourself – don't recognize your tender places and bruised spots – you will be all the more surprised when someone else recognizes them. And someone will.

Practise tenderness in your personal life; and in your work life. Ethics are not optional. Greed is not acceptable. The hoarding tendency of the Dragon will leave you lonely and sad – so keep it checked. If you have more than you need, give it away. Open your arms, and open your heart, and open your mind. And go forth, Dragon, and prosper.

LIFE PATH NINE
THE HERMIT

$$1 + 2 + 3 + 4 + 5 + 6 + 7 + 8 + 9 = 36$$

$$3 + 6 = 9$$

*

$$9 \times 9 = 81$$

$$8 + 1 = 9$$

*

$$111, 111, 111 \times 111, 111, 111 = 12345678987654321$$

$$1 + 2 + 3 + 4 + 5 + 6 + 7 + 8 + 9 + 8 + 7 + 6 + 5 + 4 + 3 + 2 + 1 = 81$$

$$8 + 1 = 9$$

In you, all things are as one. You have been here before; and everything is yours. Your life is full and rich; your inner life perhaps the most of all. You understand everything, and everyone. Perhaps you don't always admit it. What would admitting it gain? Nobody likes a know-it-all: you know that now. You know so much...

Oh, Hermit, what can I possibly teach you?

Yours is the last path, and the hardest: yours is the path of letting go.

Yours is the path of endings, and we are coming now to the end not just of the book, but of the great cycle of life. In the number nine all others are contained; in this Life Path are contained all qualities, experiences, hopes, dreams, fears of all the others.

It has taken such work to get here; and you have done the work. You continue to do the work, even when it hurts. Especially when it hurts. Especially when you are alone.

And you can feel so lonely, sometimes; so misunderstood by people who have not seen what you have seen, struggled as you have struggled. You are not afraid, but you are tired. Perhaps you feel too tired to go on as you are. And

Every great dream begins with a dreamer.

9

perhaps that's a sign to you that you need to stop. You cannot go on like this; so go on another way. You are carrying such heavy burdens, Hermit. Perhaps now is the time to set them down. Perhaps now is the time to throw some away, and hand others to other people. Who can pick up what you're putting down? Who can help you in your quest? Yours is a lonely road, but you contain multitudes – and there are many who will help you do what you need to do. Give them a chance to carry this for you, whatever this looks like.

You have earned so much, and learned so much. So can you now release what you have learned back to the wind? Can you now put that love, that learning back into those who come after?

You stand on the stage, an older, wiser Magician.

Your card is The Hermit, of course, a man standing with a lantern, a star and a staff. He is alone, at the top of a great mountain he has already climbed. He has climbed, and climbed alone, through storms and snow, through good times and bad, and now he turns inward to the self.

He is the patron of self-discovery, self-knowledge and, within that self-discovery, a sense, through his own deep wisdom, of the fact that the self is the universe; the universe is the self. He is connected to everything. All things are connected to and through him: through you.

And this, Hermit, is what you must remember – for your task is to let go. Let go of material things, let go of the things that shape you, and open yourself up to the unknown. Let it go; you are everything, and everything is you. Your sense of self, so carefully burnished and harnessed through so many lives, is only in the way now. It's the thing that's stopping you seeing the universe as it is, and your rightful place in it. Relinquish the ties that bind you. Breathe in Breathe out. Be free.

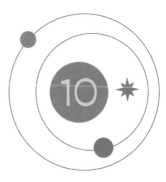

Breathe deep; breathe slow. Breathe in for a count of six; release for eight. In through the nose, and out through the mouth. Be in your body: inhale the world, and sigh it out again, the atoms of your lungs changing the atmosphere of the world around you. When a butterfly flaps her wings, somewhere a storm is created: you are both butterfly and storm, and you must live with that as best you can. Live lightly, Hermit. Today you are here; tomorrow you will be gone. How can we move with purpose in such a world? How can we go on, knowing life is a brief candle, that the Moon comes after the Sun, that the Sun comes after the Moon, and one day both will shine down on a world where we no longer live?

Your challenge, Hermit, is to let go. This is no easy task. We want to hold onto what we love, and what we are. But change is inevitable. That you have seen through your life. And change comes for everyone, and you have changed, and change has taken from you, and change has given to you…You must not just embrace change when it comes, but seek it out. You must make the changes now, today, that make you more free. You must slip the surly bonds of Earth, as the poet had it, and what that looks like only you can say.

You know the masculine and feminine, and you can take what you wish from each one. You know that gender is what you make it; that love is what you make it; that life is what you make it. You are wise beyond your years; you are unafraid of everything.

Your quest here, I suppose, is to learn to be unafraid of fear.

You cannot rid yourself of fear. Fear is natural, and fear is healthy. But you can learn to embrace it. Embrace terror. Embrace change. Embrace, even, pain.

Your quest here is to learn to be unafraid of fear.

5

Embrace it all: embrace every brief moment on this fickle, fleeting Earth. The taste of good food , the touch of a loved one, the Sun coming from behind a cloud or a torrential summer storm. Warmth. A cup of tea. Life is a patchwork of grief and joy, of sorrow and love and wild searing loneliness; of moments of such ecstatic gladness and perfect peace and sinking dread all stitched together into a great blanket that holds us all in warmth and tender care. It is a patchwork of time and space; a patchwork of energy and repair and decay. It is a tapestry. And it is, perhaps, a curtain: a curtain hanging over a stage.

8

You were the Magician, once. You were the Magician, dazzling and poised to begin in a single spotlight. Remember? You were the Magician, and a Dreamer of Dreams; a Teller of Tales; a Master of Crafts. You were a Free Spirit, a Homemaker, a Searcher, a Dragon hoarding gold and sharing wealth. You are all these things – as we all are, as we all can be and will be. You are all of us, and you have been everything, starting in a single spotlight on a stage.

And now, a new curtain, hiding a new stage, shrouded in darkness: a greater stage than any of us have ever seen. What might we bring to a new cycle? What songs, what dreams, what stories? What homes might we build, what knowledge might we find, what golden treasures might we discover?

Hermit, bring down the curtain with your great staff. Hang your lantern high, and show us the stars.

Take a deep breath. Show us the future. We begin again.

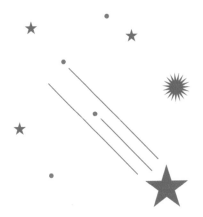